Pen to Profit

Write, Publish and Build

Pen to Profit: Write, Publish & Build

Published by CEO Wife Publishing

www.theceowife.com

ISBN for Paperback: 979-8-9897762-0-7
ISBN for E-book: 979-8-9897762-1-4

Dedication

To my family, cherished readers, and beloved community of storytellers,

Your unwavering support and endless inspiration have been the guiding light of my journey. This book is a testament to transforming your knowledge, skills, and expertise into a practical guide that empowers others on their path.

The wisdom we gain from the experience, the joy of sharing our stories, and the impact we create through writing books are immeasurable. My wish is that this book serves as a catalyst to propel you forward, personally and professionally, in your book-writing and business-building endeavors.

Peace and Blessings,

Dr. Tamara Mitchell-Davis

Table of Contents

Introduction

Welcome to "Pen to Profit": Write, Publish & Build – a transformative journey that intertwines the art of writing with the strategic prowess of business building. My life's work has been about empowering others. Lately, that focus has specifically turned towards the community of aspiring authors, leaders, and entrepreneurs who desire to write, share their stories, and transform their writing aspirations into tangible realities.

In this book, I'm inviting you on a unique adventure. It's more than just about writing a book and sharing a story. It's about crafting a legacy, building a thriving business, and changing the trajectory of your life financially, mentally, and holistically. I guarantee you that what you're about to learn will not only inspire you to create a compelling manuscript but also to strategize a flourishing business model post-publication.

As we embark on this journey together, I encourage you to show up fully. Don't just read, but take action and set the ball rolling on your path to becoming an author. In the following chapters, you'll discover the foundational steps and stages of transforming your pen's power into profit. We'll delve into the art of storytelling, the science of audience attraction, and the strategy of system implementation. Each chapter is a building block, from step one of writing your ideas to step fourteen of establishing your author brand and beyond. It is not just about reading and hoarding information. It's about doing, implementing, and executing the insights and strategies you learn. With each chapter, I'll lay out three key points or questions for you to consider, providing a structure that makes the content digestible and actionable.

Your journey to writing success and business endeavors begins now. Are you ready to turn the page and step into a world of endless possibilities? I hope so. Let's begin this exciting adventure together!

Embracing the Dream Amidst Life's Whirlwinds

My journey into the world of writing was neither straightforward nor swift. It was a path marred by fear and uncertainty, a journey that spanned almost a decade before my dream materialized into my first published book. To give you a quick backstory, growing up in the projects, dealing with poverty, life struggles, and survival, the world of authors and storytellers seemed distant and unattainable.

However, writing was my sanctuary, my solace. From a tender age, I found refuge in words, pouring my emotions and thoughts into the pages of my diary. I always believed I had a story to share, a narrative that could inspire and help others. So, I started to pen down words and develop my skills as an author even from that time.

But life, with its unpredictable twists and turns, often pushed my dream to the back burner. Then, as a young adult, I navigated through the complexities of being a single mother, experienced the highs and lows of marriage and divorce, and faced financial hurdles, including bankruptcy. These experiences, while challenging, shaped my resilience and determination. Amidst these trials, my aspiration to become an author remained steadfast, a desire and goal that I clung to. While I could not actualize it in that instant, I felt the right time would eventually come, and I needed to prepare to seize the opportunities when they would come my way.

Overcoming Fear and Doubt

Fear was a constant companion on this journey. Fear of the unknown, self-doubt, and confusion about the process often paralyzed me. Questions like "Where do I begin?" and "What should I write about?" plagued my mind, echoing the uncertainties many aspiring writers face.

But within me burned a desire to prove to myself, more than anyone else, that I could transcend these fears and manifest my vision into reality. I knew that I could write if I let go of my insecurities, fear, and self-doubt. Eventually, I did!

The Turning Point

The year 2017 marked a pivotal moment in my life. That was the year I published my first book. What started as a passion project years prior slowly evolved into a thriving business. I realized that my experiences, both the struggles and victories, held valuable lessons that could empower others.

I also discovered that I was not the only one struggling to get my story written and voice heard. I learned that so many people have the desire to write but do not have the necessary knowledge to transform their message into a book that would be a profitable source of income for them and a blessing to others. I decided to dedicate myself to guiding aspiring authors, especially women, through the labyrinth of writing and publishing.

Building a Community

I embarked on a mission to nurture a community of storytellers and dreamers. Hosting events, facilitating trainings, developing products and services, and creating a supportive network became my new calling. As I witnessed the growth and success of others, I found immeasurable satisfaction and a sense of accomplishment.

The community helped me build a network, reach others, and guide them down the path I had learned to walk through easily. It was also a place where I found fulfillment.

Trusting the Process

Throughout this journey, a particular scripture resonated deeply with me: Jeremiah 29:11, "For I know the plans I have for you." This verse became a source of strength and reassurance, reminding me to trust in God's plan and my abilities. It taught me the power of faith, both in a higher power and in oneself.

To those who find themselves riddled with doubts and questions, know that the topic you desire to write about might be common, but your story is unique to you. I, too, have walked the path you tread, faced the fears you feel, and asked the questions you ponder. Let my story be a testament to the power of perseverance, that even the loftiest dreams can be achieved with unwavering determination and trust in oneself. Remember, every great accomplishment starts with the decision to try, and every journey begins with a single, albeit uncertain, step forward.

Let's Dispel Some Book Myths

Myth #1: "Only famous or established authors can write a book."

Reality: This myth suggests that writing a book is reserved for well-known individuals or experienced authors. Anyone with knowledge, passion, and a story to share can write a book. Writing expertise can be developed through practice, guidance, and dedication.

Myth #2: "Writing a book requires a massive time commitment."

Reality: Many aspiring authors hesitate to start writing because they believe it will consume all their time. While writing a book does require commitment, it doesn't mean you have to give up everything else in your life. By creating a realistic writing schedule and setting aside dedicated time each day or week, you can make steady progress toward completing your book. We'll show you how time constraints don't have to be insurmountable obstacles on your writing journey.

Myth #3: "You have to be an exceptional writer to write a book."

Reality: The misconception that only exceptional writers can write a book can be discouraging for many aspiring authors. While having strong writing skills certainly helps, it's not a prerequisite for writing a book. Writing is a craft that can be honed through practice, editing, and working with professionals like editors and proofreaders to polish your manuscript. We'll reveal how exceptional writing skills are developed through practice and dedication and that your voice can resonate with readers regardless of your initial proficiency.

Myth #4: "Writing a book guarantees instant success and wealth."

Reality: It's important to manage expectations regarding the outcome of writing a book. While some authors achieve great success and financial rewards, it's not a guarantee for everyone. Writing a book should be driven by a passion for sharing knowledge and experiences rather than solely focusing on monetary gains. A book can open doors to new opportunities and help establish credibility and authority in your field, but the results vary for each author.

We'll dive deep into the misconception that writing a book guarantees instant success and wealth. While we celebrate the triumphs of accomplished authors, we'll emphasize the intrinsic value of sharing your knowledge, making an impact, and creating your own opportunities that can help you build your author platform.

Myth #5: "Writing a book is a solitary journey."

Reality: The image of a solitary writer toiling away in isolation is a prevalent myth. However, writing a book involves collaboration, support, and feedback from various sources. Working with other people can enhance the quality of your book and provide valuable insights.

Along your authorpreneurial journey, you'll discover the power of community, collaboration, and professional support. From engaging with fellow writers to seeking feedback and guidance from editors and industry experts, you'll realize that you're never alone on this transformative voyage.

These book myths have shackled countless passionate individuals, stifling their dreams of becoming successful authors and influential business leaders. But fear not; we're here to dismantle these misconceptions and pave the way for your triumphant authorpreneurial path.

Prepare to rewrite the narrative surrounding book writing and authorpreneurship. Let's cast aside these five book-writing myths, embrace the truth, and unlock the boundless potential that awaits you as an authorpreneur.

So, if you desire to write, create a movement with your message, and make an impact, I encourage you to believe in your dreams, take notes, process the information shared, and get ready to move from pen to profit as I walk you through each step of the process.

PART 1

Getting Started

Writing, Publishing, and Marketing Your Book

Chapter 1

The Art of Writing: Turning Ideas into Words

Every bestselling book begins with a single idea – a spark of inspiration. However, there are many sparks of inspiration in the world that will never turn into actual books. Why? Because these would-be authors never stopped to create a plan that would transform the idea into actual words on pages that could be a source of inspiration and a blessing to others.

This chapter will transform that spark into a structured plan, aligning your actions with your vision. Let's embark on laying the foundational stone of your book, a journey that begins with introspection and strategy.

Identifying Your Core Message

What is your book's core message?

Your book's core message is its heartbeat. It's what you want your readers to remember long after they turn the final page. Reflect on your experiences, expertise, and the unique perspectives you bring to

11

the table. For instance, in my book "Goodbye Fear, Hello Destiny," the core message was about overcoming internal barriers to unlock one's true potential. Find out what experiences you have had that would make your book different from any other book in the market addressing a similar subject.

Action Step: Write down three key experiences in your life that have profoundly shaped you. How do these experiences relate to the message you want to share?

1. ....

....

....

2. ....

....

....

3. ....

....

....

....

Understanding Your Audience

Who are you writing for, and what are their needs?

The success of your book hinges on how well it connects with your readers. Are you writing for aspiring entrepreneurs, seasoned professionals, or individuals seeking personal growth? For example, in my book "Dream Your Plan, Plan Your Dream," I targeted individuals yearning to translate their dreams into actionable plans. Who your audience is will affect your style of writing, marketing, and several other factors in the writing journey. Therefore, it is essential to know and understand your target audience.

Action Step: Create a profile of your ideal reader. What are their challenges, aspirations, and interests? How does your book provide solutions or insights they seek?

....

....

....

....

....

....

....

....

....

....

....

....

....

....

....

....

....

....

....

....

....

....

Structuring Your Book

How will you guide your readers through your book?

A well-structured book is like a map guiding your readers through your narrative. Start by outlining the key chapters and the flow of content. This roadmap will keep you focused and ensure that each chapter aligns with your core message. In my book "#GoalGetter," the structure was designed to take readers through a journey of self-discovery and goal setting while sharing some of my life's challenges along the way.

Action Step: Sketch a basic outline of your book. What are the major sections or chapters? How does each contribute to your overall message?

Incorporate examples and case studies, if applicable. Including real-life examples and case studies can significantly enhance your book's impact. They provide practical insights and help readers relate to the content. In my workshops, I often share stories of authors who started with a simple idea and turned it into a bestseller, emphasizing the power of perseverance and strategy.

....

....

....

....

....

....

....

....

....

....

....

....

....

....

....

....

....

....

....

....

....

....

....

....

....

....

....

....

....

....

....

....

....

....

Action Step: Identify at least two examples or case studies relevant to your book's content. How do these stories illustrate your key points?

....

....

....

....

....

....

....

....

....

....

....

....

....

....

....

....

....

....

....

....

....

....

....

....

....

....

....

....

....

....

....

....

....

....

....

....

....

....

....

....

Writing a book is a journey that requires patience, dedication, and strategy. By focusing on these foundational elements, you're not just writing a book, but you're crafting a tool that will open doors to new opportunities and growth.

The path from pen to profit begins with these first steps, laying a solid foundation for your book and the business it will inspire.

Chapter 2

Building Your Writing Muscle

Congratulations on laying the groundwork for your story and book! Now, it's time to bring those ideas to life through the art of writing. Remember, showing up every day to write is more than a practice. It's a commitment to your dream.

Let's dive into the process of turning your thoughts into compelling words!

Establishing a Writing Routine

Consistency is key in the writing process.

Establishing a writing routine sets the stage for productivity and progress. In my journey, setting aside dedicated time each day for writing was instrumental for me and for my coauthors in completing books like "Blessed Not Broken," "Love, Business & Marriage," and "Becoming Her."

Action Step: Decide on a writing schedule, whether daily or weekly, by realistically assessing the number of hours you can commit to writing. Mark these in your calendar as non-negotiable writing sessions. Write down your schedule and put it in a visible spot where you'll see it daily to remind yourself of your commitment.

....

....

....

....

....

....

....

....

....

....

....

....

....

....

Creating Your Writing Environment

What environment makes you feel most inspired and productive?

Your writing environment can significantly influence your creativity and focus. Whether it's a quiet home office, a bustling café, or a serene park, find a space that resonates with your writing spirit. For me, sitting at the dining room table or on the couch in my office is where the magic happens. I turned off my cell phone and social media notifications. I keep a glass of water nearby, set my alarm for 90-minute sprints, and just start typing away. This pattern became my routine, and eventually, my mind and body became conditioned to this practical writing time and routine.

Action Step: Identify and set up your writing space. Gather all necessary tools – your laptop, notebooks, inspirational objects, and anything else that aids your writing process. It is time to start writing.

Writing Techniques and Tools

How do you want to write?

Various writing techniques and tools can support your process. Some writers prefer free writing to let ideas flow, while others swear by detailed outlines. Explore tools like writing software, voice-to-text applications, or even traditional pen and paper to find what works best for you.

Action Step: Experiment with different writing techniques and tools. Choose the method that makes your writing process smooth and enjoyable. Write it down here so you can keep it in mind as you write.

....

....

....

....

....

....

....

....

....

....

....

....

....

....

....

....

....

....

Overcoming Writer's Block

Writer's block is a common challenge, but it's not insurmountable.

Even the best of us faces writer's block. The key is not to let it derail your progress. So, when the flow of words seems to halt, remember simplicity and familiarity are your allies. You can play around with the parts of your writing that you find easier to write. That is why it is essential to have an outline of your book from the beginning. You can go back to foundational principles in chapter one and create an outline for your book if you didn't before.

I will share some techniques to help you face writer's block. Techniques like taking a short break, switching to a different section of your book, or engaging in a different creative activity can help reignite your inspiration.

Here's an example:

Think of writing as creating a PowerPoint presentation. This approach breaks down the process into smaller, more manageable parts. Each slide in a presentation represents a key point or idea. Similarly, each paragraph or section in your writing can be tackled as a separate, concise unit. This method helps organize your thoughts and maintain a clear focus, making the writing process less daunting.

Draw on what you already know. Write about concepts and experiences you're familiar with. This technique eases the writing process and, at the same time, adds authenticity and depth to your work. In my experience, writing about topics I'm passionate about, like empowering aspiring authors or sharing business insights, naturally flows and feels less like a task and more like a conversation.

Remember, writer's block is just a temporary pause, not a full stop. By changing your approach and focusing on familiar ground, you can navigate through it and continue your writing journey with confidence and clarity.

Action Step: When you hit a block, switch to the PowerPoint presentation approach or focus on topics you're deeply familiar with. This shift in perspective can reignite your creativity and keep the words flowing. Start with what you already know and research additional information after and as needed.

Crafting Your First Draft

Your first draft is about getting your ideas down on paper. It doesn't have to be perfect. Think of it as the clay from which your final masterpiece will be sculpted. When I was writing "Dream Your Plan, Plan Your Dream," the first draft was a rough map that eventually led to a well-structured guide for turning dreams into reality.

Embrace this phase of your journey with enthusiasm and an open mind. Each word you write brings you closer to your goal of not just writing a book and sharing your story but creating a legacy. Let me repeat: it does not have to be perfect or permanent when starting, which is why it is called a first draft. Release some of that pressure and focus on the why of your book.

Why are you writing your story?

Why are you publishing a book?

Why is this information/topic important for your audience?

Turn your book-writing dream into a reality, one word at a time!

....

....

....

....

....

....

....

....

....

....

....

....

....

....

....

....

....

....

....

....

....

....

....

....

....

....

....

....

....

....

....

....

....

....

....

Chapter 3

Hiring a Professional Editor: The Strategic Approach

Securing a professional editor is a pivotal step in your authorial journey. You might think you know what you are doing and have a good command of the language, but the truth is, even the most experienced writers have editors. That's because the role of an editor is more than correcting your grammar or helping you to get your book ready to publish.

As a multi-published author, I understand the importance of an editor and the need to have a reliable one on your side. This chapter is dedicated to guiding you through the intricate process of finding and hiring an editor. This decision can significantly elevate the quality and appeal of your book.

Understanding the Role of a Professional Editor

An editor does more than correct grammar. They enhance the flow, clarity, and structure of your manuscript. Their expertise can be the difference between a good book and a great one. Recognize that your editor is a vital partner in your journey to the marketplace.

No matter how good you are at writing, there is always the blind emotional factor when you read your writing. A professional editor can spot the errors better as they are detached from the work. They can also help you see areas that need improvement in your book.

Your editor can also help you in cutting out excesses (fluff) from your book. It is essential to understand that your editor always has your best interests at heart. They want you to become the author of a great book because it's also a reflection of their work and expertise. So, think of your editor as a partner in your writing process.

The Art of Choosing an Editor

Knowing how closely a writer and editor should work on a book, you don't want to pick just anyone to be your partner on your writing journey. When selecting an editor, it's essential to consider several key factors to ensure a fruitful collaboration.

Their experience should resonate with your book's genre, as this alignment in background and interest can greatly enhance the editing process. You don't want to have an editor who doesn't understand the goal you are trying to achieve with your book. Editors who have worked on similar books can help you write a better book.

It's also wise to review their past projects to get a sense of their editing style and how it might apply to your work. If you don't like the output of any of the other books they have worked on before, it might be a pointer to the fact that they may not be the best choice to partner with you on your project.

Compatibility in communication is another critical aspect. You want to ensure that your interaction styles are harmonious for effective collaboration. If you don't find it easy to communicate your book ideas with your editor or they don't respond to you in time, it might unnecessarily elongate the editing process. Find an editor that suits your communication style.

Finally, don't hesitate to request a trial edit. This test can serve as a valuable litmus test for their suitability for your project. While the response might simply be a yes or no, it's a crucial step to take. So, go ahead and ask. You might be pleasantly surprised by what unfolds.

The decision-making process of getting an editor for your book can seem stressful, but it doesn't have to be. Trust your instincts, but also be methodical in your approach. The right editor should resonate with your vision and can elevate your voice authentically.

Finding the Right Editor

Finding the right editor for your book takes time, research, and work. It would be best if you found someone who fits all your criteria and works well with your personality. While it can sometimes be stressful, it is not impossible. You only need to know where to start. Here are some proven avenues to start your search.

- **Fiverr and Upwork:** These platforms offer a diverse pool of editorial talents. Ensure that you take your time to weed through the numbers, though. It will also do you good to stick to the platform rules in these market spaces. There are several subpar editors out there, including those who are only trying to scam you for your money. Following the platform rules can help you avoid these kinds of people. Be sure to also check reviews.

- **Referrals:** Leveraging your network can lead to trusted and vetted professionals. You can check within your community of writers and friends to find an editor that would do a good job. This method can minimize the risk of giving your book to an unqualified editor.

Making Your Editing Process Work

Securing the services of a professional editor who understands their craft and building a healthy relationship with them is essential to ensure the success of your book's editing process. This collaboration with a seasoned, skilled editor and effective communication will undoubtedly pave the way for the creation of that top-shelf book you aspire to achieve.

Budgeting for Quality

Editing is an investment. While being mindful of your budget, remember that skilled editing can exponentially increase your book's value and appeal. Find the balance between going for a quality editor and staying within your budget.

When you compare the prices of professional editors in your vicinity, you can get a good price within your budget. Never forget that prices are not the best proof of an editor's expertise. There are expensive editors who may not do a thorough job, less expensive editors who do a phenomenal job, and vice versa. Establish a budget, do your research first, understand that editing is an investment, and make the best choice based on the information you have acquired.

Fostering a Productive Relationship

Clear communication and mutual respect are the foundations of a fruitful editorial relationship. Set clear timelines and be open to feedback. It would be best if you worked with an editor that can meet your deadlines and deliver quality results.

You should also be clear to your editor about your method of communication and expected deliverables. Note that your editor is not going to know what you want your book to look like magically. You will have to be as clear as possible about everything from the beginning of your editing relationship.

Crafting Your Editor Acquisition Plan

Getting an editor is a step-by-step process. If you rush through any step, you might not get the results you want. Here's a plan to ensure you're on the right track.

- Develop a Checklist: Create a checklist for your ideal editor based on the criteria mentioned. Include aspects like budget, experience, communication style, and specific needs related to your genre. You can do a simple pros and cons list like the one below to weed through the prospective editors.

EDITORS	PROS	CONS
Ex. Melissa The Editor	Good references; Price within budget; Highly recommended; Several jobs within the same genre	Took a few weeks to respond to my email

- **Research and Reach Out:** Use your checklist to evaluate potential editors from various platforms and through referrals. Reach out to them with clear questions and requirements.

For starters, here are a few questions to ask a prospective editor...

1. **What is Your Editing Experience and Background?**

- It's essential to understand the editor's experience, especially in relation to the genre or style of the book. This question will help gauge whether their expertise aligns with the specific needs of your project.

2. Can You Provide References or Samples of Your Work?

- Asking for references or samples gives insight into their editing style and the quality of their work. This is crucial for gauging whether their approach is suitable for your book.

3. How Do You Approach the Editing Process?

- Every editor has a unique approach. Understanding their process, including how they handle feedback, revisions, and communication, will help you determine if their style matches what you're looking for.

4. What is Your Turnaround Time and Availability?

- Aligning schedules is key. Knowing the editor's availability and how long an editor typically takes to edit a manuscript will help plan the publication timeline.

5. How Do You Charge for Your Services?

- Understanding the editor's fee structure (whether it's hourly, per word, or a flat rate) and what the fee includes (like the number of revisions or follow-up consultations) is vital for budgeting and avoiding any surprises.

Decision-Making: After your research and preliminary discussions, take a moment to reflect. Which editor aligns best with your vision, budget, and style? Make your decision with both your intuition and facts in balance.

Your choice of an editor is a defining step in your book's journey. Approach this task with a strategic mindset, ensuring that your decision is well-informed and aligned with your book's ultimate vision.

By following these steps, you are not just hiring an editor, you are establishing a partnership that will bring out the best in your book and set you up for success in the publishing world.

Chapter 4

Book Formatting: The Next Step in the Process

What makes a book perfect is that extra quality that is added after it has gone through formatting.

Book design, often referred to as book formatting or typesetting, is a crucial phase in your publishing journey. It's the art of arranging your manuscript into a readable, attractive layout, preparing it for the eyes of eager readers.

This chapter will navigate you through the intricacies of book design, offering guidance on hiring help and considering the possibility of your editor providing this essential service.

The Significance of Book Design

A good book design is not just aesthetic. It ensures readability, enhances the reader's experience, and reflects the professionalism of your work. It's about making your book visually appealing and easy to read.

If your book needs images or illustrations, it is at this stage that these features are added. For certain books, it is the book design that distinguishes the book from any other book in the market. If you are targeting children, I cannot overemphasize the importance of having an attractive book design.

No matter how good the content of your book is, if the title and design don't attract people to pick it up and read it, the purpose of the book might be defeated. If you want people to read your book, invest in having an appropriate book design.

Exploring Your Options for Book Design

When it comes to book design, you're presented with a variety of options, each catering to different needs and skills. Professional design services are readily available on platforms such as Fiverr and Upwork, where a multitude of skilled book designers (freelancers) are just a click away.

Another convenient option to consider is inquiring whether your editor offers additional design services. This option can provide a seamless transition from the editing phase to formatting and design, ensuring consistency and ease. It can also be a better choice because your editor already understands your book well and would be able to provide a catchy design for your book.

For those who prefer a hands-on approach, DIY (Do It Yourself) software tools like Adobe InDesign and Scrivener offer the opportunity to undertake the design process personally. However, this option demands both time and a certain level of design expertise. Each of these paths offers unique benefits, and the choice largely depends on your specific needs, budget, and skill set.

Hiring a Book Format Designer

Deciding to hire a professional book format designer is a significant step in your publishing journey, and it's important to make an informed choice. Start by considering the experience and portfolio of potential book format designers.

It's crucial to find someone who has worked in your book's genre and possesses a portfolio that aligns with your vision for the book. This criterion ensures that the format designer understands the nuances and expectations of your target audience.

Don't underestimate the value of referrals and reviews. Reach out to your network for recommendations or explore reviews on freelancing platforms where these designers may be listed. It can give you insights into their reliability and the quality of their work.

Assess the compatibility of the format designer's style with your book's theme and personal preferences. The designer's approach should resonate with your vision and enhance the overall appeal of your book. A harmonious collaboration between you and your designer is key to creating a book that not only looks professional but also captivates your intended audience.

Integrating Editing and Design

In the scenario where your editor also offers format design services, it's beneficial to carefully weigh the advantages and disadvantages of integrating these two critical stages of book production. On the plus side, opting for a package that combines editing and format design can lead to more streamlined communication.

Since your editor is already familiar with your work, it can translate into a deeper understanding of how to complement the narrative of your book visually. This approach might also offer potential cost savings compared to hiring separate professionals for each task.

However, there are cons to consider. If your editor's primary expertise lies in editing rather than design, you may encounter limited design options. Their skills in design might not be as developed or diverse as those of a dedicated book designer. This con could mean that the final design might not fully capture the essence or potential of your book's visual appeal.

Therefore, it's crucial to carefully assess your editor's design capabilities and compare them with your expectations for your book's aesthetic before deciding.

Understanding the Basics of Book Format Design

When delving into the realm of book format design, it's essential to have a grasp of the fundamental design elements that can significantly impact the readability and aesthetic appeal of your book.

Typography plays a crucial role. The type of font you choose and its size should be easy on the eyes, facilitating a comfortable and engaging reading experience. Equally important are the margins and spacing within your book. Adequate margins and well-considered spacing not only contribute to an uncluttered layout but also ensure ease of reading, making the text approachable and legible.

Furthermore, attention to detail is key when it comes to chapter headers and footers. These elements should be consistently styled throughout the book, contributing to a professional look and feel. By paying close attention to these key design elements, you can greatly enhance the overall quality and reader appeal of your book.

Creating Your Book Format Design Plan

Once you have decided to proceed with your book formatting and typesetting, you need to determine whether you will use the services of your editor or want a separate format designer for the role. Proper research and comparison of the options you have will help you make an informed decision. You should review the portfolios and testimonials of all the book format designers.

Setting a realistic budget can also help you make a choice. However, do not forget that a well-designed format will make your book stand out, so set an adequate budget. Once you get different choices of book format designers, ask for a sample layout to gauge the designer's suitability.

Remember, the layout of your book is as critical as its content. A well-designed book format not only captivates but also retains readers' attention. Take the time to choose the right design approach for your book, ensuring it reflects the quality and essence of your work.

Through careful planning and thoughtful decision-making, you can ensure that your book not only tells a compelling story but also presents it in a visually appealing and professional manner.

Chapter 5

Crafting a Captivating Book Cover: Your Book's First Impression

Have you ever caught yourself reaching for a book just because its cover looks interesting? Well, you won't be the first reader or the last to do this. "A book is judged by its cover." This adage holds significant truth in the world of publishing.

Your book cover is not just the first impression but also a crucial marketing tool. The right book cover can make a world of difference. It's often the deciding factor for a reader choosing between your book and another. Therefore, you must ensure that your book makes the right impression on your target audience.

Hiring a professional book cover designer is an investment in your book's success. This chapter guides you through creating an eye-catching cover that resonates with your book's content and target audience.

Elements of an Effective Book Cover

Creating an effective book cover involves several critical elements that can significantly influence a reader's first impression.

1. Visual Appeal

Visual appeal is paramount. In a crowded market, a cover that stands out is not just desirable; it's essential. This aspect is where the magic of typography and formatting comes into play. The book's title and the author's name should be clear, readable, and aesthetically pleasing, ensuring they catch the eye of potential readers.

2. Alignment

Another vital aspect is the cover's alignment with the content of the book. The design should encapsulate the essence of your book's content, giving a hint of the journey that awaits the reader inside.

3. Audience Appeal

Always consider your target audience in the design process. The cover should be tailored to appeal visually to your specific audience, resonating with their preferences and expectations.

By focusing on these elements, you can create a book cover that is not only visually striking but also effectively communicates the heart of your book to your intended audience.

Understanding ISBN

The ISBN, or International Standard Book Number, plays a crucial role in the world of publishing. It serves as a unique identifier for your book, making it an essential tool for efficient marketing and distribution. This unique code helps catalog and track your book across various sales channels and libraries.

It's important to ensure that your ISBN is prominently included on the copyright page to maintain the professionalism and accessibility of your book. ISBN can also be found on the back cover of the book. Acquiring an ISBN is a straightforward process

Image Source: Shutterstock

In the United States, authors can obtain it through a platform like Bowker (my identifiers). If you're outside the U.S., you'll need to contact your local ISBN agency. This process not only legitimizes your book but also facilitates its distribution and discovery in the vast world of literature.

Hiring a Book Cover Designer

Like the process of looking for an editor, your book cover designer plays an essential role in your book journey. You can take the following steps to hire the right designer.

- ***Search for Talent:*** Platforms like Fiverr, Upwork, or specialized design services offer a range of designers.

- ***Check Portfolios:*** Look for designers with experience in your genre and a style that resonates with you.

- ***Read Reviews and Seek Referrals:*** Recommendations from fellow authors can be invaluable. Remember to read reviews and check references, if applicable.

Planning Your Book Cover Design

Define your vision for your book cover design. Note down key elements you want on your cover, including style, colors, and imagery. You should also research and shortlist designers based on your vision. Find designers who align with your needs. Clearly convey your vision and content to the designer for an effective book cover design process. You should also set a budget, remembering that a quality cover is an investment in your book's future.

Your book cover is more than just a protective layer. It's a visual story, enticing readers to delve into the pages. By choosing the right book cover designer and effectively communicating your vision, you can create a cover that not only grabs the attention of your target audience but also accurately represents the heart of your book.

Embark on this journey with clarity and creativity, ensuring that your book not only shares knowledge but also visually communicates its value to your audience.

Chapter 6

Navigating the Self–Publishing World: Your Path to Publication

Embarking on the self-publishing journey is an exciting and empowering process. This chapter aims to guide you through the nuances of self-publishing, providing valuable insights into resources and strategies that have worked for many, including myself.

This chapter is your roadmap to self-publishing success, from choosing the right platform to leveraging your book for greater financial and personal gain.

Choosing the Right Self–Publishing Platform

There are several platforms for self-publishing, each with its unique benefits. You can search online, and you will get an abundance of options. Here are a few popular ones that I've used:

- Amazon Kindle Direct Publishing (KDP): Easy to use, with a vast audience reach.

- Lulu: Offers great print options and wide distribution channels.

- IngramSpark: Renowned for its quality printing and extensive distribution network.

Understanding the Pros of Self-Publishing

Self-publishing presents a range of advantages that can be particularly appealing to authors. One of the most significant benefits is complete creative control. As a self-publishing author, you have the autonomy to make all key decisions about your book, from its content and cover design to its marketing strategy. This level of control ensures that the final product aligns perfectly with your vision.

Self-publishing often leads to higher royalties compared to traditional publishing routes. Since no traditional publishers are involved, you retain a larger portion of your book's sales, enhancing your potential earnings.

Another advantage of self-publishing is the ability to reach the market swiftly. This route is typically faster than traditional publishing paths, allowing your book to reach readers more quickly. Once your book is ready, you don't have to take it through a ton of processes as it can be when publishing with a firm.

Self-publishing also offers flexibility. You have the freedom to update your book as needed and publish it on your schedule, which is a luxury not often afforded in traditional publishing. This flexibility can be a significant asset in the rapidly evolving world of publishing.

Maximizing Your Financial Returns

To maximize your financial returns as an author, consider employing a couple of strategic approaches. First, focus on direct sales. By selling your books through your website and at events, you can keep a more significant portion of the profits. This direct-to-consumer approach enhances your earnings and allows you to build closer relationships with your readers.

Alongside direct sales, it's crucial to leverage online marketing. Utilizing social media platforms and online marketing strategies can significantly broaden your audience reach. Effective online marketing boosts your book's visibility and drives sales by targeting and engaging potential readers across various digital platforms.

Combining these two strategies — direct sales and robust online marketing — can be a powerful way to increase your book's financial success.

Self-Publishing Plan

Explore different self-publishing platforms and compare their services and costs. Define what success looks like for your book – whether it's sales numbers, reaching a certain audience, or something else.

Develop a strategy for promoting your book, including leveraging your website and social media. Have a budget for your publishing, and consider the costs of self-publishing, including editing, book cover design, and marketing.

Self-publishing is a journey that requires dedication, but it is incredibly rewarding. You can successfully navigate the self-publishing world by understanding the landscape, choosing the right platform, and strategically planning your publication and marketing. This chapter lays the foundation for you to take control of your publishing journey and achieve the success you envision for your book.

Chapter 7

Mastering Book Presales, Marketing & Launching

Marketing a book isn't just an activity that starts post-publication. It's a journey that begins the moment you conceive your book idea. The mistake many aspiring authors make is waiting until all aspects of the book are ready before doing any form of marketing.

This chapter is dedicated to guiding you through the art of book presales, marketing, and launching, ensuring your book not only reaches your audience but also makes a significant impact.

Seeding Your Book – Planting the Idea Early

"Seeding" is the process of subtly introducing your book idea to your audience well before the book is published. It involves sharing the journey, teasing content, and engaging with an audience.

You can do this by regularly updating your audience on the writing process, sharing snippets or themes to pique their interest, and using their feedback to shape your book and marketing strategy. You can make use of social media and community gatherings for your "seeding."

This marketing ensures that the interests of your target audience are already piqued before you even have half of the book ready. It is this strategy that makes the book sell out at launch. Let your target audience in and let them follow you through the process and journey of writing. The anticipation can only work in your favor.

Book Presales – Selling Before Launch

Presales are crucial for building momentum. They involve setting up pre-order options, offering incentives, and tracking your progress. You can utilize platforms like Amazon or your website to take pre-orders.

If you go the website route, I suggest having a professional headshot, book cover, a short summary about the book, a professional (short) bio, and your payment processor connected so you can drive traffic there and accept payments. You will need to keep track of books sold, so once you have the copies in hand, you can ship them directly to those customers who purchased from you.

Regarding incentives, you can give bonuses like signed copies or exclusive content to pre-order customers. Use presale numbers to gauge interest and adjust your marketing strategies accordingly.

Building Momentum and Buzz

Creating a buzz is about activities that increase awareness and hype from ideas to make your book launch a significant event. Strategies include social media campaigns, email marketing, and influencer collaborations. You can utilize these strategies by posting regular, engaging content about your book on your social media platforms.

Utilize email marketing to share updates, teasers, and offers exclusively with your email list. You can also partner with influencers to reach a broader audience. Anything that gets people talking about your book in a positive light is a good thing.

Pre–Launch, Launch, and Post–Launch Strategies

Navigating the crucial stages of your book's journey—pre-launch, launch, and post-launch—requires a strategic approach, blending meticulous planning with engaging, actionable steps. This systematic yet dynamic process not only maximizes the impact of your book but also ensures a seamless transition through each critical phase of its unveiling.

Pre-Launch Stage

The pre-launch stage is your opportunity to generate buzz and anticipation. Begin by crafting and sharing captivating teasers of your book, like a thought-provoking chapter excerpt or an intriguing quote, across your social media platforms and email newsletters.

Next, establish pre-order options on various platforms, coupling them with enticing incentives like exclusive bonus content or signed copies for early buyers. Make your presence felt in the media by appearing on podcasts, local radio shows, or guest blogging, especially in forums that resonate with your book's theme. For instance, if your book is centered around leadership, you can share leadership insights on a relevant podcast, subtly plugging your upcoming release.

Action Step: Reflect on the key message of your book and create a teaser that would captivate your audience's curiosity. Think about an incentive that would encourage pre-orders. Identify at least one media outlet where you could share insights related to your book's theme. Write down the teaser idea and media outlet here. Now, take action to implement and execute this idea and put it into practice repeatedly.

....

....

....

....

....

....

....

....

....

....

....

....

....

....

....

....

....

....

....

....

....

....

....

....

....

....

....

....

....

....

....

....

....

....

Launch Stage

The launch is a celebration of your efforts and creativity. Plan an engaging event, whether virtual or physical, making it an experience to remember for your audience.

During the event, ensure an active online presence, engaging with your audience in real-time and encouraging attendees to share their experiences on social media. Feature special segments like a live reading or a Q&A session to generate additional interest and online buzz. Have copies of your book on hand; be sure to capture the moments with photography and videography that you can later use/repurpose for marketing content.

Action Step: Envision your ideal book launch event. What unique elements would make it memorable? Draft a plan for engaging with your audience online during this event.

....

....

....

....

....

....

....

....

....

....

....

....

....

....

....

....

....

....

....

....

....

....

....

....

....

....

....

....

....

....

....

....

....

....

....

Post-Launch Stage

Post-launch is about maintaining momentum and keeping your book in the public eye. Actively encourage and share reviews on various platforms, and continue making media appearances to discuss your book, linking it to current trends or discussions. Repurpose the content and footage you captured during the launch stage.

Consistently update your marketing efforts, perhaps by hosting monthly online discussions or events related to your book's themes, keeping the conversation alive and engaging with your audience. When applicable, take pictures with customers as they are purchasing copies of the book. It will help build social proof that you can keep sharing and repurposing with your audience and the audience of your customers to expand your reach.

Action Step: Think of innovative ways to encourage reviews for your book. Plan a media appearance or an event that could keep the discussion around your book alive post-launch.

....

....

....

....

....

....

....

....

....

....

....

....

....

....

....

....

....

....

....

....

....

....

....

....

....

....

....

....

....

....

....

....

....

....

....

....

....

....

....

....

....

....

....

By following these steps with dedication and creativity, you launch a book and create an enduring narrative and connection with your audience, ensuring lasting success and impact in the literary world while building relationships, community, and book awareness.

Building and Leveraging an Email List

Building and leveraging an email list is pivotal in establishing your author platform. A compelling case study illustrates this: an author experienced a significant 30% increase in presale numbers simply by regularly engaging their email list with updates and exclusive previews. This example, highlighted in the article "The Power of Email Marketing for Authors" by Smith Publishing (2021), underscores the importance of maintaining an active and engaging email strategy.

Another example: According to data from Constant Contact, email marketing brought returns of $36 for every dollar spent, making it one of the most effective marketing channels available.

Rather than just using emails as a tool for sales pitches, the key is to offer genuine value to your subscribers. This technique can be achieved through sharing behind-the-scenes content, offering sneak peeks of upcoming works, or providing insights into your writing process. By nurturing your email list in this manner, you bolster presale figures and forge a stronger connection with your readers, laying a solid foundation for your author platform.

https://blog.allauthor.com/email-marketing-for-authors/

Collaborations and Partnerships

Collaborations and partnerships in the world of book publishing are a powerful way to expand your reach and enhance your book's success. These alliances can take various forms, from partnering with organizations, influencers, or other authors for cross-promotion. The benefits are many.

Collaborations enable you to tap into your partner's audience, effectively broadening your reader base. This exposure to a new group of potential readers can significantly boost your book's visibility and sales. Partnerships often lead to a pooling of resources, be it in marketing, distribution, or expertise, allowing for more efficient and impactful promotional efforts.

In essence, collaborations and partnerships in the book industry are not just a strategy for increasing sales. They are a means to foster community, learning, and growth, all of which are crucial for a successful and fulfilling authorial career.

Master Your Book Marketing

Beginning your marketing as soon as your book idea forms is critical. This initial phase isn't about aggressive selling but about sparking interest and building awareness. Share the evolution of your book, from concept to creation, to weave a captivating narrative that draws in your audience from the very beginning.

Engagement with your audience is the next crucial step. Use every platform at your disposal—be it social media, email lists, or direct interactions—to forge a strong, meaningful connection with your readers. This engagement should extend beyond just promotional content; it's about sharing stories, insights, and experiences that resonate on a deeper level with your audience, making them feel a part of your book's journey.

Finally, the power of partnerships cannot be overstated. Collaborating with influencers, bloggers, and businesses can significantly extend your reach to new audiences. These collaborations should be mutually beneficial, providing value to both parties involved. Through joint promotional efforts, guest blogging, or co-hosting events, these strategic partnerships can greatly enhance the visibility and appeal of your book.

By integrating these strategies—beginning your marketing early, engaging deeply with your audience, and leveraging strategic partnerships—you'll craft a comprehensive marketing approach that not only boosts your book's success but also solidifies your brand as an author.

A successful book launch is about much more than just writing a great book. It's about strategically marketing and creating a buzz around your book from the moment you conceive it.

PART 2

Building With Your Book

Your Book Is Your Business

Chapter 8

Building Your Author Platform

Embrace Your Unique Voice

I guarantee you that you have a story to tell. Building a strong author platform starts with embracing your unique voice and story. Don't try to be like other people in your niche. You don't have to be a carbon copy of what others are doing. Be innovative and creative in your approach. Someone out there needs your message, so be okay with thinking outside the box and exploring different ideas with the goal and intention of getting your story into the hands of those who need it most.

If you want to build an author platform that will stand the test of time, you need to be authentic in your writing. I am not saying that you cannot learn from others. But don't let what others have said or have to say about your work change you. You can shine with your book if you are true to yourself.

Show up authentically in every piece of content you create. Whether it's your blog, social media posts, or your books, let your personality shine through. This authenticity is what attracts your tribe.

Consistent and Engaging Content

Consistency is key to building an audience. Ensure that you're sharing valuable, relevant content consistently. It could be blog posts, videos, or podcasts – whatever medium resonates most with you and your audience.

The world acknowledges and rewards those who stick to what they do. Even if you don't have the numbers you want yet, keep showing up, and in due time, the engagement will increase.

If you think you are doing something wrong in your audience engagement or marketing strategies, you can take some time to re-evaluate and pivot but don't disappear forever. You never know who is watching and waiting on your content.

Building Relationships & Connections

Networking is crucial. Connect with other authors, thought leaders, and influencers in and outside of your niche. Expand your connections. Participate in online forums and engage with your audience. Don't be a ghost member of your online communities.

Remember, it's not just about selling books. It's about building relationships. Go to events within and outside of your niche, and when you do, don't just sit in a corner. Talk to people around you. You never know who you might meet. It could be someone who will inspire your next book or co-write it with you. Start building relationships with like-minded and like-interested people. Network, Network, Network!.

The ABCD's of Your Client Journey

Understanding your client's journey is absolutely vital, especially in the realms of coaching, consulting, and personal development, where individualized paths and experiences are paramount. By understanding each client's unique journey, you can tailor your advice, strategies, and solutions to fit their specific needs and circumstances. Here's how you can start identifying where your client is on their journey:

A for Advocates

Advocates are your champions. They've worked with you, believe in your message, and are walking billboards for your brand. They're your success stories, the ones who sing your praises to anyone who will listen. Nurture these relationships – they're gold!

B for Budding Connections

These are individuals who know you well. There's a relationship, but it's not yet at the business stage. Your goal? Deepen these connections. Share valuable insights, engage in meaningful conversations, and show them how your work can elevate their lives.

C for Casual Contacts

These people know you through your content or communications but haven't engaged deeply yet. The key here is to draw them in. Provide compelling content, invite them to webinars or workshops, and showcase the value you offer.

D for Deferred Prospects

Deferred prospects are potential customers who aren't ready yet. They're aware of you but need more time or information. Patience and persistence are your tools here. Keep providing value, stay on their radar, and when they're ready, they'll come to you.

Moving Clients Through the Stages

The journey from D to A isn't just a funnel. It's a nurturing process. Each interaction is a step closer to turning a deferred prospect into a loyal advocate. Engage, educate, and empower them at each stage.

Example: Imagine a prospective client at point D – they've heard of you but haven't engaged with your brand yet. Your book becomes the entry point. Here's how you guide them through the journey:

1. Initial Engagement (Point D to C): Offer your book as a gateway to your expertise. For instance, let's say you meet Melissa at a networking event. She's heard of you but hasn't engaged with your services. You offer her a copy of your book at regular price, discounted, or as a gift for attending the event. This gesture nudges Melissa from a deferred prospect (D) to a more engaged contact (C).

2. Building the Relationship (Point C to B): After Melissa reads your book, follow up with a personalized email or message. Ask for her thoughts and offer additional resources that align with her interests or challenges. This personal touch and value-add move her closer to a business relationship (B).

3. Deepening Engagement (Point B to A): Now that Melissa is familiar with your work and has interacted with you, invite her to an exclusive webinar or a small group coaching session. This interaction allows her to experience your expertise firsthand. Offering a special discount to book readers for these sessions can be a great incentive.

4. Creating Advocates (Point A): Once Melissa experiences the transformative impact of your coaching or services, she becomes more than just a client; she's an advocate. Encourage her to share her success story. This share could be through a testimonial, a social media post, or by referring others to your book and services. Her advocacy solidifies her loyalty and attracts new prospects to begin their journey at point D.

This action step emphasizes the power of personal connection and the strategic use of your book as a tool for engagement. By nurturing each relationship and offering tailored value at every stage, you can effectively move clients through the journey from initial awareness to loyal advocacy. Remember, it's about aligning your actions with your client's needs and making it a priority to engage them at every step.

Chapter 9

Crafting Your 5K Blueprint

Diversify Your Offerings

Diversity is key to reaching that initial 5K goal. Mix it up with books, coaching programs, courses, and speaking engagements.   Let's say you set the price of your book at $20. Selling 250 books will net you $5,000. But don't put all your eggs in one basket. Remember, it's not just about quantity but the value you bring to your audience.

Leveraging Smaller Achievements

This 5K blueprint is about more than just financial gains. It's a stepping stone. Each book sold, every workshop conducted, and each program you run contributes to building your reputation and authority. These achievements pave the way for bigger milestones.

In this journey, remember the importance of nurturing relationships at every level, from deferred prospects to devoted advocates. Each interaction, sale, or enrollment is a vital part of the larger picture. You're not just aiming for a financial goal – you're building a community and a legacy.

Strategic Pricing and Sales

Consider introducing a mix of products and services. For instance, a smaller workshop or online course priced at $500 would only require 10 participants to reach your goal.

Sample Breakdown for 5K

Let's visualize a scenario: You sell 150 books and enroll seven clients in a $500 program. That's 150 x $20 (book sales) + 7 x $500 (program enrollment), totaling $5,500. Here, you've not only met your 5K goals but also added a bit extra!

Now, let's consider a 10K goal.

High-Value Programs

Consider offering a high-value program or workshop. If you price a program at $1,000, you only need to sell to 10 prospective clients to reach a 10K goal. Combine this with your book sales, and you've got a winning formula.

Sample Breakdown

Imagine this: You sell 100 books and enroll nine clients in your $1,000 program. That's 100 x $20 +

9 x $1,000, equaling $11,000. You've not only reached your 10K goal, but you've also surpassed it!

You have the ability and opportunity to transform lives – one book, one program, one connection at a time.

Now, what is your goal?

....

....

....

....

....

....

....

....

....

....

....

....

....

Conclusion

Congratulations on reaching the end of this enlightening journey! You have bravely confronted the five book-writing myths, read through the steps to take your book from an idea in your head to a book in your hands, see what it takes to get your book ready for self-publishing, and learn how to build your author platform and grow your business with a book.

Writing a book is not an exclusive club reserved for the famous or the naturally gifted. It is a craft that can be cultivated and honed through perseverance, dedication, and a willingness to learn. As an authorpreneur, you possess a unique blend of entrepreneurial spirit and storytelling prowess that can propel you to new heights of success.

In addition, the true value of writing a book lies in the connections you make, the expertise you share, and the doors it opens to new opportunities. Embrace the journey and the personal growth it brings, knowing that the impact you make on readers' lives is immeasurable.

Now, armed with the knowledge and inspiration gained from these pages, it's time to put pen to paper (or fingers to keyboard) and bring your story and book to life. But before you embark on the writing exercises that follow in the appendix, remember this: your words have the power to change lives, shape industries, and leave a legacy. So, go forth, authorpreneur, and make your mark on the world through the transformative power of your book.

The world is eagerly waiting for your story, your wisdom, and your unique perspective. Once you are published, your book can position you as an expert in your industry, add credibility and authority, allow you to attract clients, create an additional stream of income, help you build brand awareness, and grow your business. So, stay the course and continue the path from pen to profit!

Wishing you boundless creativity, unwavering determination, and an incredible authorpreneurial journey ahead!

About Me

Dr. Tamara Mitchell-Davis is a multi-bestselling and award-winning author celebrated for her compelling approach to storytelling and her deep-rooted passion for empowering others. As the CEO of TM Davis Enterprise, LLC, she harnesses the power of words and strategic thinking to uplift aspiring authors, coaches, and entrepreneurs, guiding them to bring their book and business visions to fruition.

Holding a master's degree in business administration and a 085 School Business Administrator Certification from the State of Connecticut, Dr. Tamara blends her academic prowess with a natural flair for narrative to create impactful works. Her published books to date in 2023 are each a testament to her storytelling expertise and motivational style. They include:

1. #GoalGetter: Strategies for Overcoming Life's Challenges - A guide to navigating life's hurdles with determination and grace.

2. Goodbye Fear, Hello Destiny- An empowering call to embrace one's true potential by shedding fears.

3. Dream Your Plan, Plan Your Dream: 7 Steps to Manifesting Success - A strategic roadmap for turning dreams into reality.

4. Blessed Not Broken (Vols.1, 2, 3, 4, and 5) - A series that explores resilience and finding strength in challenges.

5. Love, Business & Marriage - Insights into harmonizing personal and professional life for entrepreneurial couples.

6. Becoming Her - A journey of self-discovery and personal evolution.

7. Coauthor in Dear Momma - A collaborative work celebrating the complexities and beauty of motherhood.

Dr. Tamara's 'why' lies in her belief in the transformative power of storytelling. She sees each story as a unique opportunity to connect, inspire, and empower individuals to realize their potential and make meaningful changes. Her dedication extends beyond writing, as evidenced by her founding of the Pen to Profit: Write, Publish & Build community on Facebook, hosting the annual Pen to Profit Conference, and creating her very own Podcast.

Some of her accolades include the 100 Women of Color for Leadership and Community Service,

ACHI Magazine Orator of the Year, I AM Her Woman of Influence, and CEO of the Year, to name a few, which reflect her impact and commitment to elevating others.

Dr. Tamara's media appearances span several platforms like Women of Distinction Magazine, Voyage Dallas Magazine, Canvas Rebel, Black Women Mean Business, and more, showcasing her thought leadership and influence. As an active member of Delta Sigma Theta Sorority Incorporated, she contributes to her community, embodying the values of service, sisterhood, and leadership.

Residing in Connecticut with her husband and children, Dr. Tamara continues to write, speak, and inspire. To secure her for speaking opportunities and embark on a journey of growth, storytelling, and success, you can connect with her at www.tamaramdavis.com.

Appendix A

Quick Steps for Turning Pen to Profit

Step #1: Clarify your Purpose

- Why are **YOU** writing the book?

- What is the main goal of your book? Do you want to educate, inspire, or provide practical tips?

- Who is your ideal reader? Are you targeting young or seasoned professionals, entrepreneurs, or a specific niche in your industry? Basically, think about who will benefit the most from reading your book.

Step #2: Brainstorm Book Ideas

Don't stay in stuck mode - start with what you already know.

- What are you passionate about?

- What information can you share?

- Brainstorm and write down your ideas.

Step #3: Choose your Best Book Idea

- If you could only write ONE book or share ONE story, which one would it be?

Step #4: Market Research and Outlining

To ensure your book resonates with your audience and stands out in the market, research what you don't know and create a book outline for organization and focus.

- Conduct market research to identify existing books on similar topics. Analyze their content, style, and unique selling points.

- Outline your book's structure, including chapters, subtopics, and key takeaways. It will serve as your roadmap throughout the writing process.

Step #5: Develop and Write Engaging Content

Your content should be informative, engaging, and tailored to your audience's needs. Consider the following strategies:

- Start with an attention-grabbing introduction that hooks the reader and clearly states the book's benefits.

- Share relatable stories to illustrate concepts and make your content more relatable.

- Incorporate practical exercises, worksheets, or checklists to help readers apply the concepts you're discussing, if applicable.

- Use a conversational tone to create a connection with your audience and avoid jargon whenever possible.

- When you write, don't edit. Don't worry about typos or grammar- just write.

Step #6: Structure and Organization

The organization of your book plays a crucial role in delivering your message effectively.

- Ensure a logical flow from one chapter to the next. Each chapter should build upon the previous one and lead seamlessly to the next.

- Use clear headings and subheadings to guide readers through the content.

- Consider incorporating chapter summaries or key takeaways to reinforce the main points and help readers retain information.

Step #7: Ask someone to write your book's foreword (if applicable - optional)

Step #8: Alpha Readers

- Choose someone you "trust" to review manuscripts for flow, content, and consistency to ensure you are communicating the intended message. Feedback should be given back to you within a week.

Step #9: Editing and Proofreading

Editing and proofreading are crucial steps to polish your book and ensure its quality.

- Read through your manuscript and fix typos. Pay attention to the clarity and coherence of your writing, making necessary revisions to improve the overall flow.

- Consider hiring a professional editor or asking trusted colleagues to review your work and provide feedback. There are different forms of editing - be sure to ask questions and gain an understanding of the "services(s)" to be provided.

Step #10: Design and Formatting

Investing in professional book cover design and book formatting will enhance the visual appeal of your book.

- Books are judged by the cover. Hire a professional book designer to create an eye-catching cover that aligns with your book's content and target audience.

- Use appropriate typography and formatting styles to ensure readability.

- Incorporate visuals, such as graphs or charts, to enhance the presentation of complex financial concepts.

- ISBN (International Standard Book Number) - The purpose of the ISBN is to establish and identify one title or edition of a title from one specific publisher and is unique to that edition, allowing for more efficient marketing of products by booksellers, libraries, universities, wholesalers and distributors (www.isbn.org). ISBN should be included on the copyright page of your book.

Step #11: Beta Readers

- Share the final manuscript with someone you trust. Request review(s) of the book.

Step #12: Publishing and Distribution

Selecting the right publishing and distribution channels is essential for getting your book into the hands of your target audience.

- Consider self-publishing through platforms like IngramSpark or Amazon Kindle Direct Publishing. Do your research. There are several to choose from.

- Upload the manuscript, book cover, and other essential information to the desired publishing platform.

- Order a draft copy to review the entire book from cover to cover to ensure it looks and reads as you desire.

- It's NOW ready for your desired audience (readers).

Step #13: Marketing and Promotion

Once your book is published, it's time to promote it effectively and maximize its visibility:

- Plan a launch party/ book signing.

- Develop a comprehensive marketing plan that includes online and offline strategies.

- Create a professional author website or landing page to showcase your book and engage with potential readers.

- Utilize social media platforms to build an author platform, share valuable content, and connect with your target audience.

- Seek opportunities for guest blogging, podcast interviews, and speaking engagements to establish yourself as an expert and generate interest in your book.

- Encourage reader reviews and testimonials to boost credibility and attract more potential readers.

Step #14: Establishing Your Author Brand

Beyond the book itself, focus on building your author brand and positioning yourself as a go-to authority in your industry:

- Consistently create valuable content through blog posts, articles, or newsletters that align with the theme of your book.

- Engage in networking events, conferences, or industry associations to expand your professional connections and visibility.

- Leverage your book as a marketing tool for speaking engagements, workshops, or consulting opportunities.

Lastly, think outside the box and explore all the possibilities and opportunities you desire.

Appendix B

I want to leave you with a glimpse into an exciting new development – a tool that I am currently crafting to take your author journey to extraordinary heights. This tool is the A.U.T.H.O.R. framework, an innovative approach to guide aspiring authors like you through the intricate dance of writing and business building.

The A.U.T.H.O.R. framework stands for:

A = Articulate Your Vision

U = Unleash Your Story

T = Transform Writing into Action

H = Harness Your Platform

O = Optimize Your Business

R = Reach More Prospective Clients

This framework is not just a methodology; it's a journey into the heart of what it means to be a successful author and entrepreneur. Each element represents a vital step in the process of not only writing a book but also transforming it into a cornerstone for your business and personal growth.

Are you intrigued? Do you feel the stirrings of excitement at the thought of what the A.U.T.H.O.R. framework might hold for you? If so, I invite you to stay connected. This framework is more than a teaching tool; it's a gateway to transforming your aspirations into tangible realities. Stay tuned!